Huntsman Spiders

Huntsman Spider Pet Owner's Guide

Huntsman Spider's breeding, where to buy, types, care, temperament, cost, health, handling, diet, and much more included!

By: Lolly Brown

Copyrights and Trademarks

All rights reserved. No part of this book may be reproduced or transformed in any form or by any means, graphic, electronic, or mechanical, including photocopying, recording, taping, or by any information storage retrieval system, without the written permission of the author.

This publication is Copyright ©2019 NRB Publishing, an imprint. Nevada. All products, graphics, publications, software and services mentioned and recommended in this publication are protected by trademarks. In such instance, all trademarks & copyright belong to the respective owners. For information consult www.NRBpublishing.com

Disclaimer and Legal Notice

This product is not legal, medical, or accounting advice and should not be interpreted in that manner. You need to do your own due-diligence to determine if the content of this product is right for you. While every attempt has been made to verify the information shared in this publication, neither the author, neither publisher, nor the affiliates assume any responsibility for errors, omissions or contrary interpretation of the subject matter herein. Any perceived slights to any specific person(s) or organization(s) are purely unintentional.

We have no control over the nature, content and availability of the web sites listed in this book. The inclusion of any web site links does not necessarily imply a recommendation or endorse the views expressed within them. We take no responsibility for, and will not be liable for, the websites being temporarily unavailable or being removed from the internet.

The accuracy and completeness of information provided herein and opinions stated herein are not guaranteed or warranted to produce any particular results, and the advice and strategies, contained herein may not be suitable for every individual. Neither the author nor the publisher shall be liable for any loss incurred as a consequence of the use and application, directly or indirectly, of any information presented in this work. This publication is designed to provide information in regard to the subject matter covered.

Neither the author nor the publisher assume any responsibility for any errors or omissions, nor do they represent or warrant that the ideas, information, actions, plans, suggestions contained in this book is in all cases accurate. It is the reader's responsibility to find advice before putting anything written in this book into practice. The information in this book is not intended to serve as legal, medical, or accounting advice.

Foreword

Usually the Australian Huntsman Spider is only purchased by newbies and enthusiasts alike out of mere curiosity. However, most often than not, Huntsman spiders surprises new keepers because of its many interesting behaviors! If you ever thought that pets are only limited to the tarantula species, and all – time favorite spiders like the barking spider, jumping spiders, wolf spider etc. you are quite mistaken. Reconsidering other lesser known species like the Huntsman can perhaps give you utmost delight!

Huntsman spiders are quite big, quite hairy, have eight set of eyes and eight legs (you know, like a usual spider) but the thing that separates them to the common itsy bitsy spiders is their super long legs and fearsome reputation!

Although this spider species appear dangerous and venomous (mostly because of their unusually long leg span), I'm happy to say that they are not, which is why experts recommend them as pets. However, they are still known for their aggressiveness, agility, and piercing bite – things that usually freak a non – enthusiast, and perhaps shock a newbie keeper. They are not venomous but if they are taunted or perhaps mishandled they will not hesitate to bite you.

The Huntsman spiders are sometimes responsible for the shrieks and shudders among the non – keepers, and most often than not, they are treated as pest not pets. Despite of being a notoriously known as a 'biter,' and/ or a 'monster' to some people, their fearsome reputation is not really necessary.

Get ready to hunt and learn how the Huntsman spider can teach you a thing or two about always getting on your feet – and perfectly landing on them! This book will guide you on how to acquire, keep, and take care of them as household pets.

Table of Contents

Introduction 1

Chapter One: Biological Information of Huntsman Spiders . 5

    Variations of Huntsman Spider Species 6

        Brown Huntsman Spider (*Heteropoda jugulans*) 7

        Badge Huntsman spider (*Neosparassus spp.*) 7

        Green Huntsman spider (*Typostola barbata*) 7

        Grey Huntsman spider (*Holconia immanis*) 8

    Huntsman Spiders in Focus... 8

    Huntsman Spider Facts and Physical Features 10

    Behaviors of Huntsman Spiders 13

Chapter Two: Huntsman Spiders as Pets 17

    Threats to Huntsman Spiders.. 18

    Acquiring Permit.. 19

    Should You Keep More than One? 20

    Costs of Keeping a Huntsman Spider.................................. 22

    Pros and Cons of Keeping Huntsman Spiders 23

Chapter Three: Hunting the Huntsman! 27

    Steps on How You Can Acquire a Huntsman 28

    Do's and Don'ts of Choosing a Huntsman Spider 32

Chapter Four: Housing the Huntsman Spider 35

    Reminders when setting – up a cage.................................... 37

Chapter Five: Handling the Huntsman and Common Behaviors 43

    Huntsman Spiders Behavior 44

    Tips for Handling Huntsman Spiders 48

Chapter Six: Feeding Your Huntsman Spiders 53

    Nutrition for your Huntsman Spiders 54

        Feeding Adults 54

        Feeding Slings 55

    Feeding Frequency 55

    Dos and Don'ts of Feeding 56

    Materials to Use When Feeding Huntsman Spiders 58

Chapter Seven: Breeding Your Huntsman Spiders 61

    Tips to Prepare Your Huntsman Spider for Breeding 62

    The Mating Process 64

        The Courtship 64

        The Ritual 65

        The Mating 66

        Incubation and Egg – Laying 67

Chapter Eight: Frequently Asked Questions 69

Chapter Nine: Top 10 Spider Myths 77

Chapter 10: Summary and Care Sheet 85

Index 99

Photo Credits 103

References 105

Introduction

People that are not spider hobbyist find Huntsman spiders as something really freakish especially whenever they just pop at the house out of nowhere. However, if you're a spider enthusiast, you'd probably be amazed at how quick these spiders are on their feet and their range of behaviors that you wouldn't find in other friendly species.

They are called Huntsman spiders because they are free roaming species, and they are notoriously agile, aggressive, and powerful whenever they are trying to capture a prey, something that a real huntsman would do. They usually prey on small size creatures like roaches, crickets, moths, beetles, and other insects.

Introduction

Compared to other spider species, Huntsman spiders have a different method of capturing their prey, although they produce silk, they don't build webs to trap their food. They just do it like a real 'huntsman' through using their legs, fangs, and good ol' hunting powers. They usually use their silk just to build their house, protect their eggs, and act as safety lines in case a predator tries to pounce on them.

In their native land of Australia, there are over 200 species of Huntsman spiders and a whole lot more is not yet discovered or studied. These creatures' original habitat are deserts, sub – alpine areas, and rainforests. If ever you find them popping in your house all the time, it's probably because you are the one residing on their environmental 'house' and not the other way around, so I guess, you're the one trespassing, not them. Some species of Huntsman spiders are common in wide areas while others are limited to small areas in their native country.

This spider species are not venomous although some wild ones, usually those that come from their native land in Australia, possess some mild venom but even if that's the case, their venoms are still not considered fatal for humans; the Huntsman spiders being sold in pet stores or from a backyard breeder are (and should) be non – venomous. However, it's best that you still ask the breeder if such species do so that you're aware of it when it comes to keeping and handling one.

Introduction

Contrary to popular belief, spiders including this one are usually reluctant to bite and they don't chase people even if it appears that way. Believe it or not, their act of climbing walls or jumping onto you is totally unintentional. It's just that their weird looking legs and their agile movement are most often than not mistaken for 'aggressiveness' when in reality, these poor creatures are just trying to escape from any perceived danger.

Spiders don't see things like we do, even if they have a set of eight eyes on them, and they also can't see people or any creature from a distance which is why they are extra careful whenever they're out and about because they have no idea if predators will attack them from a distance. If you see your Huntsman spider jumping or crawling fast towards you, that's a sign that they are attempting to get away from you, paradox isn't it? This species is not recommended for newbie keepers but if you are the type of person who wants to have an "action – packed" and 'interactive' pet then the Huntsman spider is definitely the way to go. Get to know more about their way of living on the next few chapters!

Introduction

Chapter One: Biological Information of Huntsman Spiders

This eight legged critters that make people shriek share an eternal love and hate relationship with us humans and also our ecosystem whether we like it or not. Despite their hairy and creepy appearance, many of them including the Huntsman are pretty harmless although the bite could definitely sting like a bee. Still there are lots of spider species out there that are quite venomous but those kinds are usually found in the deep jungles or in the wild. Just like sharks in the ocean, these eight legged critters play an important role in our ecosystem but it's quite understandable that some people just don't like to be anywhere near them.

Chapter One: Biological Information of Huntsman Spiders

Of all the 40,000 spider species in the world, the Huntsman spider is feared perhaps the most undeservingly, and it's mainly due to its agile abilities and crab – like legs. In this chapter, you'll learn in depth about this creature including its extraordinary appearance and abilities. See if the Huntsman is the kind of pet spider you want to have in your collection.

Variations of Huntsman Spider Species

Huntsman spiders are arboreal creatures which mean that they are comfortable if they're up in the air or hanging in your walls. However, they can still adapt living upon the ground or flat surfaces like tree trunks, branches, or the terrarium you're going to provide for them.

They are large and long – legged creatures that usually come in grey and brown colors. They are also quite distinct because their legs are banded.

Other Huntsman spider species like *Delena* (which is the flattest), *Holconia, Isopedella, and Isopeda* have flat body structures that are well adapted for residing in small or narrow spaces such as under rock crevices or loose barks. They can live in such tight spaces because they have the ability to bend their legs vertically in relation to their body. They can also twist their joints that they spread out laterally in a crab – like manner. On the other hand, the *Heteropoda*

Chapter One: Biological Information of Huntsman Spiders

(brown – colored Huntsman), and *Neosparassus* (badge huntsman species) have less flattened bodies.

Brown Huntsman Spider (*Heteropoda jugulans*)

The brown – colored huntsman species has a light motley brown pattern. They are usually found in houses and the mother spider often times leave their egg sacs in pipes causing young huntsman spiders to come out in the bathroom.

Badge Huntsman spider (*Neosparassus spp.*)

These huntsman species are called "Badge" because of their shield – colored pattern. They have striking yellow, orange, black, and red colors that are hidden underneath their abdominal area. The upper part of their body sports an even yellow and brown color, and their head is smooth.

Green Huntsman spider (*Typostola barbata*)

Green Huntsman species actually sport a more fawn – colored body than green. However, these creatures do have a green colored leg joints, and you can find a greenish colored area throughout their body. They also possess black

Chapter One: Biological Information of Huntsman Spiders

dots on their abdominal area. They are known as timid, and some of them have an orange – looking moustache (patches of hair) between their fangs.

Grey Huntsman spider (*Holconia immanis*)

These species sport a chocolate – brown to a black stripe color that extends halfway down their body. They also tend to be timid spiders like the Green Huntsman, and they have a flat head.

Huntsman Spiders in Focus

The Huntsman spider is believed to have originated in Sri Lanka, and southern regions of India but majority are now distributed in many regions of Australia, and even in warm areas like Florida, U.S.A. These spiders are fond of entering houses and buildings where their prey – hunting abilities are welcomed. Huntsman spiders are also known as the "Giant Crab Spider" because their 2 pair of front legs is spread out just like a guarded crab. They have incredible hunting and preying abilities even at a young age; juvenile ones can easily kill roaches, and the adults can catch lizards and even small – sized bats in the wild! They are quite ravenous indeed!

Chapter One: Biological Information of Huntsman Spiders

Huntsman spiders get to grow freakishly large but they are really not that scary as most people would think. However, as a precaution especially if you are just a newbie keeper or someone who haven't handled large spiders like this one before it's important to note that their bite will not kill you but it will sting – and they are definitely a biter.

Do keep in mind though that the reason they bite is because they feel threatened or perhaps they are mishandled. There's a possibility that their mild venom can cause some allergic reaction to some people, and there had been some cases on rare occasions that their bite could affect the central nervous system of the body. Some people experience diarrhea, vomiting, nausea, or hot/ cold chills, but people usually report that they're fine the next day, so as a precaution, try not to touch your Huntsman spider if it's not needed.

If ever you do like to play with them, I suggest you use a glove to avoid getting bitten. Do not let them be handled by your kids as well, and if you do, make sure to supervise them. As I've mentioned before, these spiders are quite aggressive in nature, though for hobbyists they'll be treated as "playful" but if taunted or if they feel uncomfortable with how you handle them, they will NOT HESITATE to bite you.

Chapter One: Biological Information of Huntsman Spiders

Huntsman Spider Facts and Physical Features

The Huntsman spider's scientific name is *Heteropoda venatoria*. They are distributed in mainland Australia, and they mostly thrive in cold regions of other countries, while some have found their homes in warmer areas. They are considered pantropical creatures or cosmo – tropical species. They can also be found in subtropical areas of United States like California, Florida, Texas, Georgia and coastal areas of South Carolina. They can also be found in some parts of Asia as some of its relatives are distributed there. Aside from being known as the Giant Crab Spider, Huntsman spideys are also called Banana Spider because of its occasional appearance in bananas that are being sold in the market.

Huntsman spiders are often times mistaken for big brown recluse (*Loxosceles reclusa*) which is a poisonous and venomous spider. However, the Huntsman is neither related to these spider species nor it is that dangerous to humans.

- Huntsman spiders are large, with a flattened body structure, laterally spread out banded legs, and usually come in brown color with slight dorsal patterns.

Chapter One: Biological Information of Huntsman Spiders

- The body of adult Huntsman spider measures 2.2 to 2.8 centimeters, or about one inch. Their leg span measures 3 to 5 inches or around 7 to 12 centimeters.

- Huntsman spiders have leg joints that are rotated backwards making the underside of their legs face forward, and it is spread out in a lateral position especially the 2 front legs resembling a crab.

- There's also a carpet of hair located on the underside of the last joints of their long legs as well as in the tips of their feet enabling them to grip on flat surfaces whenever they're climbing walls or structures, and also defend themselves against potential predators.

- They have a set of eight small eyes that are neatly arranged in two rows of four.

- The Grey – colored Huntsman and the Green – colored Huntsman are the 2 biggest Huntsman spider species. The legs of both creatures can stretch up to about 20 centimeters; the longest recorded leg span measures 30 centimeters! These creatures are quite common in Queensland which is a city in Australia.

Chapter One: Biological Information of Huntsman Spiders

- Huntsman spiders are quite recognizable because they are the only large spider species that can climb sheer vertical surfaces without falling, thanks to their crab – like legs.

- The male Huntsman spiders are quite smaller in body structure than their female counterparts but males have longer legs and a much smaller abdomen.

- Just like other spiders, male Huntsman species are easily identified because of their palps. Palps are tiny leg – like appendages that's located in between the spider's fangs and first pair of legs. This is because the tips of their palps are much visible compared to females, and it's also quite more swollen as it is used in mating.

- Both male and females possess a yellow to cream clypeus, and they have a band that encircles their carapace. The band is usually color tan in females, and cream – colored in makes.

- Males sport a dark and longitudinal stripe on their abdomen, and there's a pale area behind its eyes.

- The legs of both male and female Huntsman have black spots from each of the erectile macroseta. If you

Chapter One: Biological Information of Huntsman Spiders

can't seem to find black spots in this area, your spider's hairs may not be that noticeable.

- The disc – like egg sacs of females usually measures around 1 ½ cm in diameter. It is carried under the body and will remain immotile until such time that the female will mate.

- The development of young, juvenile and adult spiders usually occur simultaneously throughout the year.

Behaviors of Huntsman Spiders

- When it comes to mating, Huntsman spiders tend to have the longest mating time compared to most spider species. The record to beat is 10 hours! And unlike most spiders, females tend to be quite 'sweet' and 'loving' towards their mates. Most female spider species are aggressive to the males which is why the mating is often times quick. Male spiders usually tend to run off right after mating because females will try to eat them if they stick around. Well, not with the female Huntsman species!

Chapter One: Biological Information of Huntsman Spiders

- When it comes to reproduction, when the female Huntsman is ready to lay her eggs, what she'll do is spin a silk pad. She will then lay the hundreds of blue – green colored eggs into a hard web sac that she created, similar to a nest. The female will guard her eggs, and if ever you try to threaten her, she'll most definitely bite you, so please don't!

- Some huntsman spiders tend to be quite social as well compared to most species which are cannibalistic. They live in groups sometimes and usually defend their colony against other spider species. They also show maternal care towards their young.

- Huntsman spiders are highly valued especially in tropical countries because they usually feed on roaches and other pests and domestic insects.

- They are strong, fast, agile, and has powerful jaws which they all use to capture their prey. And like many spiders, they kill their prey buy injecting venom into it and sucking blood before completely consuming them.

- Huntsman spiders also adapt very well to human habitat, this is why they can be seen in sheds, roofs,

Chapter One: Biological Information of Huntsman Spiders

barns, and other sheltered areas. You can already tell that they will be just happy with the terrarium you're going to provide them.

- Some creatures are cold – sensitive, and some thrive in warmer areas. In Florida, U.S.A. they are commonly found in avocado groves.

Chapter One: Biological Information of Huntsman Spiders

Chapter Two: Huntsman Spiders as Pets

Huntsman spiders are one of the most interesting creatures in the world. According to many experts, they deserve a place in the pantheon of Australian wildlife. Under the family of Sparassidae, there are over 155 Huntsman species roaming around Australia where a large percentage is distributed. The Huntsman spiders are believed to have originated from Southeast Asia and Papua New Guinea before most of them immigrated to Australia and elsewhere. Huntsman spiders are now becoming more popular than ever especially among spider enthusiasts who are sort of looking for a more playful and interactive spider species.

Chapter Two: Huntsman Spiders as Pets

They are very aggressive when touched unnecessarily, and it's best if you have an expert guiding you because even experienced spider keepers are surprise of their sometimes wild behavior. In this chapter, you'll learn about the importance of getting a license or a permit, the pros and cons of keeping one as well as the costs and basic materials you'll need to properly house them.

Threats to Huntsman Spiders

Fortunately, compared to other more popular spider species, Huntsman spiders aren't endangered animals and there population is not exceedingly threatened by illegal pet traders. Perhaps the reason is because they are quite hard and dangerous to capture, or because they don't have that much demand due to their fearsome reputation. They maintain a relatively stable number but every now and then, they are experiencing a threat.

The usual threat to spiders is deforestation and loss of habitat. There are various reasons why these creatures suffer from such threats but it's usually because us humans are creating man – made establishments and activities at the expense of their natural habitat. Even though the population right now is stable, zoologists are still saying that their population might get threatened and endangered in the future. So if ever you see a Huntsman spider or any other spider species for this matter around your house, try not to kill them, and just leave them be especially if they aren't doing anything "freakish." Their population is very important in the ecosystem and they can also help you get rid of unwanted pests like roaches, beetles, and other insects.

Acquiring Permit

You don't necessarily need to get a permit before you can keep a Huntsman spider, but since this is considered quite an aggressive pet for most people, and their species are quite threatened, you may want to still consider getting one just for the sake of formality. The permit will of course come in handy if ever you're going out of town/ country and you want to take your pet with you.

Licensing systems are in place for these animals because it helps in the protection of wildlife from aggressive exploitation as well as the negative impacts to their population. Here are some of the other benefits:

- Licenses ensure that the populations of wild plants and animals like the Huntsman spider remain viable.

- It helps maintain in keeping, taking, using and transport of wildlife for recreational, commercial or other purposes.

Chapter Two: Huntsman Spiders as Pets

- It protects illegal collection of this species from the wild by illegal traders.

I advised that you only acquire a Huntsman spider that has been bred in captivity to dissuade unscrupulous hunters from snatching them out of their lairs. If you want to stay out of trouble and ensure that you're abiding your local laws, then it's best to check with your local animal or pet organization to determine if owning one would need licensure in your state or place of residence. This will provide further regulations regarding pet spiders and both protect you and your pet.

Should You Keep More than One?

This is entirely up to you, but I suggest you first start keeping one. Even if you're already an experienced spider keeper, handling larger species like the Huntsman spider can be quite exhausting but also rewarding at the same time. You have to also consider your budget when it comes to feeding and housing them especially if you already keep a number of spider species because the last thing you want to do is to run out of money to buy for their food.

Chapter Two: Huntsman Spiders as Pets

It's also important that you have a sufficient space especially if you plan on getting more than one Huntsman. The good thing though about these species is that they are quite communal unlike other spider types that are cannibalistic and cannot be house in the same terrarium. Even if that's the case, you should still consider the possibilities of them preying on one another which is why it's best that you first start keeping just one, and observe your pet's behavior as you go along. Monitor them and get to know what they like and don't like to see if it's possible to house another one of their kind inside.

You should also consider the climate and environmental factors designed specifically for their needs because some Huntsman prefer warmer climate while some like the cold a little bit. This is why it's important to know their personality and how they will react to certain things. The behavior and traits of the animals needs to be taken into consideration to gauge compatibility. Monitor the terrarium very closely to ensure that the temperature and overall conditions are right for your pet. At the end of the day, it's your responsibility to ensure that they are happy and safe in their little homes.

Chapter Two: Huntsman Spiders as Pets

Costs of Keeping a Huntsman Spider

Here are the things you need to consider before keeping Huntsman spiders as pets:

Purchase Price

The cost of acquiring Huntsman spider from a reputable breeder can range in price depending on its availability. You can expect to pay from as little as $8.98 for slings and as much as $70 and up for juvenile or full grown Huntsman species.

Enclosure and Cage Accessories

Huntsman spiders grown into huge species! They need lots of leg room, so to speak. This is why you may need to really invest in a good quality and large terrarium or container. However, if that's not within your budget, don't worry though because one of the major perks of keeping Huntsman spiders are that because of their ability to rotate their joints, and due to their naturally flat body structure, they can be happy residing in rock crevices and loose barks. But of course, they'd be happier if you provide them with a more spacious enclosure. Keep in mind that this is where your pet will build its house of webs, and this is the place where he/she will stay for a very long time.

Chapter Two: Huntsman Spiders as Pets

When purchasing an enclosure, make sure that it has a secure lid on top that's preferably made out of glass so that you can monitor it well. Since Huntsman spiders are arboreal pets, they would most likely want a terrarium that's quite tall to practice their 'ninja' moves. Depending on the type and size of the terrarium it can cost between $50 and $100 for full size enclosures. Glass tanks are a bit more expensive than small plastic enclosures. Small plastic enclosures are ideal for slings.

You may also want to provide cage decors inside the enclosure, one that resembles their habitat in the wild so that they can easily adjust. You may need to provide rock/ bark crevices substrate, heat pads, and plastic ornaments where they can build their webs. Do not put harmful materials inside the cage and avoid unnecessary things that will not help them in any way otherwise they can get harmed out of curiosity.

Pros and Cons of Keeping Huntsman Spiders

As interesting and fantastic as they are, Huntsman spiders may not be a good choice if you're just a newbie spider keeper. It's also not advisable for young kids to be taking care of one, not only because they are huge but also because they are notorious biters. The Huntsman spider is

Chapter Two: Huntsman Spiders as Pets

more suitable for people who already have prior experience when it comes to keeping other spider species or perhaps quite large spider creatures because maintenance can also be dreadful at times. Here are the pros and cons of owning one:

They are Big and Really Agile

There are quite a lot of small and non – endemic spider species in Australia, and many of them only weigh about 1 to 2 grams and on average such species are only as large as the palm of your hand. Then there's a golden huntsman species scientifically known as *Beregama aurea* which are found in Queensland. It weighs around 5 grams, and the forelegs have a length reaching up to 15 centimeters. The eggs that females lay are usually the size of a standard golf ball.

They are also very fast, and agile. Native Australian creatures can run up to 42 body lengths per second, while some only run for about 16 body lengths per second on average. Nevertheless, the Huntsman is some of the fastest spiders in the whole world.

This can be both a pro and a con because the main reason why lots of experienced spider keepers like them is because they're sort of "action – packed" and interactive compared to other spiders that are just lying around even if you already taunt them. However, the major con here is that

Chapter Two: Huntsman Spiders as Pets

you might have difficulties in catching them if ever they escape from their enclosures.

They have a Long Lifespan

Huntsman spiders are one of the long – lived spider species out there. On average they can live of up to 2 ½ years. They have shorter lifespan compared to primitive spiders like tarantulas that has a lifespan of 20 years. However, most spider species only last for about a year. This is another advantage because you as the owner wouldn't need to care for it for a very long time; on the other hand, you will lose your pet after 2 years of keeping them. Make every moment count!

Some Huntsman species are communal

There are social Huntsman species that can live in complex family groups; one example is the *Delena cancerides.* They can live with other 150 of their kind and is led by a dominant matriarch. Most spider species are not communal, and if you try to make them live in one enclosure; they will surely kill one another. However, some Huntsman species can live together with their own kind. According to researchers, the Huntsman spider mom usually establishes a residence of colony under a bark of tree, or some sort of a private retreat. The mom will keep her offspring (1 to 4 clutches) with her until they are about 1 years old. Having older siblings in the group is usually advantageous to younger ones because the older sibling can share a prey with them.

If you happen to acquire a *Delena cancerides* Huntsman species, you'll have no problem housing them in one enclosure because they will it to be that way. However, for other Huntsman species this may not be the case. Make sure to ask your breeder if the spiders you acquire can live together in one enclosure at least while they're still slings (young spiders).

Chapter Three: Hunting the Huntsman!

Assuming that you are already decided, and you're now ready to purchase this long – legged lightning fast creature, it's time for you to learn where to properly purchase a Huntsman spider, and how you can best acquire it. There are many seasoned spider breeders out there that can attest to the inhumane ways of illegally capturing Huntsman spider species in the wild to be sold off at a much higher price in pet trades. Buying arachnids from such pet traders is a big no – no because it will only make them do it again thus contributing to the endangerment and habitat loss of the species.

Experts and spider hobbyists alike highly recommend that you only buy slings that are bred in captivity because

Chapter Three: Hunting the Huntsman!

aside from saving their population and other environmental preservation, it will also sort of guarantee you that the sling or even adult spider you're getting was bred properly and isn't exposed to any pathogens as those caught from forests.

In addition to this, the Huntsman spider may already be traumatized by all of the process it went through in the hands of the illegal trader thus making it more aggressive and perhaps more sickly. It might also be difficult to feed, handle, and keep them because they were not used to being raised in captivity.

There are many options where you can buy cool looking Huntsman spiders but it's better to be careful and extra wary because there are usually lots of illegal traders posing as backyard breeders or hobbyists while they're selling the illegally acquired pets online. We'll give you a few reminders you need to keep in mind when buying from breeders.

Steps on How You Can Acquire a Huntsman

Follow the Experts

I highly recommend that you only buy from the experts or seasoned hobbyists because these people are really dedicated to what they do, and they're not just doing

Chapter Three: Hunting the Huntsman!

it to earn money. Many breeders will discourage you in buying from pet stores because most often than not, the species are not taken care of properly or there are some issues of improper husbandry, although of course, that's not always the case.

I highly recommended that you buy from reputable breeders to ensure that you'll get a healthy breed. Buying from them will also help conserve and protect the Huntsman spider species population. Following the experts and buying from them will also get you a mentor, and teach you tips and tricks on how to do things easily.

One of the best places to meet breeders and enthusiasts alike is by attending pet conventions and spider exhibitions. You can buy, sell, and generally network with each other regarding your common interest in Huntsman spiders. This can be a great place to find like-minded people, share your interests in a pet that may not be universally loved by everyone, and to establish great networking opportunities with breeders from whom you may buy, ask questions, and possibly even sell or trade some of your own spider species.

Chapter Three: Hunting the Huntsman!

Step #1: Ask for recommendations. It's best to read testimonials of people who have already bought spiders from specific breeders. This way you'll get to know the breeder based on an unbiased opinion. Asking for past customer's feedback and recos will make it easier for you to search the right and reputable breeder.

Step #2: Compare the recommended breeders. The good thing about our online world today is that you can immediately search everything with just one click. After taking in the advice of the people from social media or from the feedback of the breeder's customers, it's time to narrow down the list and do some more research about your top picks. You can check the recommended breeders' purchase cost, their background or About Page (if any) on their website, and see who best resonates with you.

Step #3: Compare the purchase prices and check their current stock. Never order a spider online without asking where it came from especially if the cost seems unusually high because this could mean that the spiders are hunted in the wild, sold cheap to the distributor, and passed on to the customers at double the price or more than the standard cost for that particular species.

Chapter Three: Hunting the Huntsman!

Step #4: Go and visit the breeder and the spider breeds!

After you've made your decision, you should consider whether or not you'll check the facility by visiting the breeder. This way, it will validate or further verify your assumptions, and you'll see the spiders live in action.

Step #5: Ask for proof from the breeder. If you can't visit the breeder for some reason, you can still see if they are legit through phone interview. You may also opt to ask for pictures of the breed, and if possible a video to see if you're getting the right breed.

Step #6: Be inquisitive. One sure way of knowing if the breeder you've chosen really knows what he/she is doing is through asking them questions. If they are a reputable and passionate breeder, they'll understand your inquisitive nature. They must also be polite enough to answer all of your questions, and perhaps even ask you some questions as well.

Chapter Three: Hunting the Huntsman!

Do's and Don'ts of Choosing a Huntsman Spider

Do buy a Huntsman that displays alertness and agility. Huntsman spiders are known for its agility and quick reflex, this is one of the first things you should look for when picking a spider. The Huntsman should display fluid movement when touched. It's a sign that they don't have any immobility issues or other health concerns.

Don't buy a Huntsman that is curled up. By this point, you now know that Huntsman spiders can rotate their joints and fit themselves into narrow spaces but you have to consider where they also live at the moment. If they are stored in an enclosure with enough room yet they're still curled up that could mean that they are ill.

Do consider your budget. Whenever you're buying a spider species, or any other kinds of pets for this matter, you have to consider your budget because the purchase price will vary depending on the size of the spider. Slings or baby spiders are way cheaper compared to juvenile and adult Huntsman.

Do consider your time and attention. It's also up to you whether you want to take care of baby spiders or adult spiders. Slings are more fragile, more difficult to feed, and more likely to die while molting so there's that risk, but the

Chapter Three: Hunting the Huntsman!

advantage is that you'll be able to see how they'll develop and grow. Buying adults on the other hand will mean high – level maintenance but presents an equal learning experience and the major advantage is that they do not require such delicate care compared to baby spiders, and they are generally easy to care for.

Don't buy a lethargic Huntsman. Some Huntsman species especially the adults also have a reputation for being timid but that doesn't mean that they shouldn't react to any movement or whenever you tried to touch them otherwise that could mean that they are completely lethargic. Timid is different from lethargy. The Huntsman should still possess a balance level of alertness and aggression since they are natural predators. Avoid lethargic spiders.

Don't buy unhealthy looking Huntsman. How will you know that they are unhealthy? You can check their physical characteristics. Make sure to check for any inconsistencies with their body parts or if there are any forms of discharge or injuries in their body. Make sure that they are as large and heavy as they need to be because that's also a sign that they have properly grown.

Chapter Three: Hunting the Huntsman!

Do Your Own Due Diligence. Ask the breeder if the spider has some history of illnesses or behavioral problems so that you'll know what kind of Huntsman you're going to deal with as they also have their own set of personalities. If one spider is much less of a biter than the other then by all means pick that. You don't want to have a very aggressive Huntsman.

Chapter Four: Housing the Huntsman Spider

The Huntsman spider is quite easy to care for if you already have an idea on how to prepare their habitat. A recommendation for newbie keepers is to keep your pet in a small tank which will give maximum visibility (of course this may only apply to slings or juvenile Huntsman not the full size matured spiders). Make sure that it comes with a fitted lid with sufficient ventilation, to keep the spider in its enclosure. A fluctuating room temperature in a warm home is best. Keep in mind that Huntsman spiders even if they look tough and dangerous can still acquire certain illnesses while they are in captivity, and it's generally because of poor

Chapter Four: Housing the Huntsman Spider

husbandry or insufficient diet, but most of the time it is because of unsanitary living conditions.

Part of proper husbandry is making sure that they have a clean enclosure. You don't have to clean it every day or every week. It's ideal that you do it at least twice a year so that you won't disturb them too much. Spot cleaning regularly is entirely up to you but this may not be advisable if the enclosure or tank is too big or if there are lots of ornaments inside because your spider will get disturb.

If ever you do decide to spot clean the cage, you can do this by temporarily placing your spider to another holding container. Remove all the contents of the tank, wash and sterilize the tank inside out, replace the substrate, clean the water dish, and sterilize all the items inside the tank before replacing them or putting them back.

You should also ensure that the temperatures and humidity levels are at the appropriate range. There are many cases of spiders dying from inappropriate levels of temperature and humidity. Molds or fungus could begin to grow in your pet's cage if it is too moist, this in turn could start contamination and infection on your pet. If the cage is too dry, daily misting with a substrate that holds moisture is a quick solution which is something that we will discuss later in this chapter.

Chapter Four: Housing the Huntsman Spider

Reminders when setting – up a cage

- **Buy a slightly tall enclosure for your arboreal pet.** Huntsman spiders are arboreal creatures which mean that they would prefer to stay up on their enclosure's wall. Tall kinds of cages work well for arboreal creatures especially for matured or adult Huntsman spiders. Some keepers prefer to get a horizontal size cage that is quite wider and deeper. Either way, it's best that you get a taller one because it will act as an exercise opportunity for your Huntsman since they also like to climb up and have that arboreal quality.

- **Adjust the size of the enclosure according to their age.** If you plan on acquiring a sling, it's best if you start it off with a small enclosure so that you can easily monitor its temperature and humidity. Huge enclosures will not be ideal for baby spiders, just transfer them to taller and bigger cages once they reach maturity.

- **Huntsman spiders are communal.** They are the only spider species that can stand to be around with their own kind without preying on them. However, I don't recommend you to mix up a sling with an adult one because the matured one can still be cannibalistic

Chapter Four: Housing the Huntsman Spider

towards the baby spiders. It's best if you house Huntsman spiders that are the same size or it's much better if they are siblings (meaning they have one mother/ dominant matriarch). Taller cages will also be ideal if you're trying to save up space in your enclosure so that it'll make room for others if in case you want to add more than one sling or spider.

- **Make sure to get a durable enclosure.** When it comes to durability, it's better to buy a slightly expensive one if it means that it's of good quality because it can be used for the lifetime of your pet Huntsman.

- **Buy a glass tank.** More specifically a 10 gallon glass tank. You can also buy a plastic enclosure if that's what you prefer but glass tanks are much more durable in my opinion. The downside of glass tanks is that it's quite harder to clean and/or relocate. Nevertheless, it's a good place for your pet. Make sure to also buy something that has a secure and easy to open lid (for you) to ensure that your Huntsman spider doesn't escape. You can also put a decoration or a background like a poster that you can buy from pet stores so in that way it can look nicer and can blend in at your house like a display. Getting a glass tank is much easier way for you to observe and monitor your pet spider from time to time.

Chapter Four: Housing the Huntsman Spider

- **Provide your pet with substrate.** Even if Huntsman spiders tend to just hang out at the back of flat tree barks or rock crevices, it's best that you still provide them with enough substrate as it will resemble their natural habitat in the wild. They won't spend as much time on the ground like ground – dwelling spider species but a substrate will provide humidity levels inside the cage. Try buying an orchid bark. It's a wood chip kind of substrate that's easy to clean, use, and also much cheaper compared to other types of bedding. After pouring in about 2 inches thick of bedding, you can add some coconut bedding for humidity purposes. After pouring it all in, you can start mixing them up, and ensure that the coconut bedding is properly distributed with the orchid bark substrate to form a nice layer.

- **Set up rock crevices and loose flat barks inside the cage.** Huntsman spiders love to just flatten their long legs on the wall, rock crevices, or under tree barks. That's where they set up their web and chill all day until a prey comes close to them. When setting up ornaments inside the cage, you can opt to buy a piece of tree bark that resembles a log. You can set it up in away where you can see your pet spider. Simply put the flat bark or log against the glass so that you can actually see where they are at the moment. Spiders

Chapter Four: Housing the Huntsman Spider

usually want to hide in places where its dark so make sure to put the log where the 'privacy' of your pet will not be entirely compromise. You can also choose to buy a large cork flat with like a hollow space in it, and just put it against the side of the glass so that they have other hiding options.

- **Decorate your spider's enclosure.** You can also opt to decorate your cage and also put fake plants inside it. You can buy a plant that looks real but something that will hold up in a cage even if it's submerged in there. You can also keep it clean once you do your spot cleaning. Huntsman spiders don't really need full – on decorations (the simpler, the better) but they'll surely enjoy their artificial habitat if it perfectly resembles their natural environment in the wild. Don't put too many plants or fake ornaments because it can be hard to clean if you do so.

- **Provide heat pads and thermometers.** Set up the right temperature and humidity level thermostat by providing heat pads. Make sure that the heat pad has an easy to control thermostat so that dialing down the temperature will be easy. What usually happens when you set up a heat pad is that your Huntsman spider will come out and stay in the place where the heat pad is located to keep themselves warm. You

Chapter Four: Housing the Huntsman Spider

can also opt to buy radiant heat panels if you have more than one Huntsman spider. You should also buy a thermometer to easily gauge or monitor the cage temperature and to know if the heat pad is properly set up. You can buy different kinds of thermometers in pet shops that you can easily stick at the back of the cage.

- **Regulate the temperature and humidity levels.** The enclosure should at least have a temperature of 18 to 25 degrees Celsius. The temperature will highly vary depending on where you live. If you live in a warmer region, you can keep the cage quite cool but make sure that you've provided them with a heated area to go to. Keep in mind that what you want to achieve is to mimic the humidity level of the wild inside the cage, and you can do that by providing them with a nice and humid cage. Add more sphagnum moss to increase the level. You can just set it up anywhere in the cage best if it's away from its main burrow area or perhaps on the sides of the cage. This way you can get the moss wet without necessarily destroying its web. The ideal humidity level is between 60 and 70%. Some Huntsman species will do well even in 50% level humidity.

Chapter Four: Housing the Huntsman Spider

- **Mist the enclosure every day.** Lightly spraying water into your pet's enclosure is beneficial. Should humidity levels increase too much, just try to even out the situation by leaving out any introduction of water to the space for a few days until the humidity levels are just right. Just keep in mind that the warmer you keep your Huntsman spider, the faster its metabolism will be. They will have greater appetite, and they will grow faster but this may also mean that the substrate will dry faster and they might be more prone to dehydration. Use your best judgment, and pay close attention to what seems best for your individual Huntsman spiders. Mist the cage to ensure that your pet is properly hydrated.

- **Remove any unnecessary left – overs like food or exoskeleton after molting.** Remove any exoskeleton when it finishes molting as well as any uneaten food or live preys. Uneaten foods should be removed immediately because to avoid parasite or fungus penetration.

- **Check in on them from time to time.** Make sure that you check on your spider daily to make sure that it doing the normal things it does. Inspect its enclosure and give all sundries a check, making sure to see that all is in place and is functioning as it should.

Chapter Five: Handling the Huntsman and Common Behaviors

The reason why Huntsman spiders are feared by many people and aren't usually chosen as pets is not because they are intimidating, big or because they have very long legs (honestly speaking with the exception of their crab – like legs, they do look a lot like many of their relative spiders) but perhaps because people aren't familiar with them and they don't know their behavior. Knowing the 'personality' or how the spider reacts to certain things as well as knowing about their natural abilities is essential to lessen the fear especially to those who have a phobia.

Chapter Five: Handling the Huntsman and Common Behaviors

Human handling can be shocking for these spiders which are why it's not recommended that you always handle them or disturb them especially when they're sleeping – in the morning! They might react aggressively and bite.

If you want to be a responsible spider keeper and you want to get along with your pet, you have to know their personality through research and experience because this doesn't only assure a healthy and peaceful integration with the new spider into its new habitat, but it also gives the keeper an advantage of knowing what to expect when in it comes to the behavior of its new pet.

Huntsman Spiders Behavior

Huntsman spiders are nocturnal species

They come out at night and emerge from their hidings to look out for food like insects and other invertebrates both smaller and a bit larger than their size. They are known as ambush predators, and they don't use their webs to catch their prey, instead what they do is to sit and wait before leaping onto their target food. And because of their very long legs and agile movements they usually catch their prey off guard.

Chapter Five: Handling the Huntsman and Common Behaviors

Sit and Wait Predator

Another reason why Huntsman spiders use to detect if a prey is nearby is through their vision and vibrations. Even if their vision is not as accurate as what us humans possess it still works out for them in combination of the vibrations they feel through the hairs on their eight legs. These are the things that enable them to easily and accurately catch a prey and at the same time move away from any potential predator. In this sense, you can consider the Huntsman spider as your 'army' to get rid of insects and other pests around your house and garden.

Agile at night, timid during the day.

In daytime, Huntsman spiders are considered timid unless they are taunted or threatened. If there's no one bothering them or if a prey is not around, they usually just stay and rest under rock crevices, loose tree barks, and other dark retreats. This is the reason why lots of people find these spiders behind curtains, under the bed, or in other unexpected places because narrow and tight spaces are what they usually prefer to rest in after foraging for food at night. Don't be surprise if you always seem to find a Huntsman inside your house because they are simply adapted to our

Chapter Five: Handling the Huntsman and Common Behaviors

environment and for some reason they like to hang out behind furniture.

A bit of a biter but not dangerously venomous

Whenever you do find them inside your house and you want to get rid of them, you can do so by getting a take – away container. What you can do is to simply scoop it up into the container and then release it outside. Don't kill it because that's what lots of people especially those who really have arachnophobia (fear of spiders). Don't worry because Huntsman spiders almost never bite even if they have a reputation of being a biter. They usually rely on their speed to get away from potential predators but even if they do bite you, you have nothing to worry about because usually it's just a quick nip to defend themselves but they don't usually inject their mild venoms. We will talk more about how to handle them later as well as what to do in case your pet bites you or happen to have injected the venom.

If you happen to acquire a Badge Huntsman species, you have to be a bit more careful whenever you're handling these creatures because they are known to have more potent venom.

Chapter Five: Handling the Huntsman and Common Behaviors

Discreet and shy – type creatures

Spiders in general are discreet creatures, which is why little is known regarding their communication methods. They usually meet with other species of their own kind during the mating season. Male Huntsman spiders when confronted by another male species either defend its burrow or fight for the female species. If the male can sense that the female want to mate with him, they will take their time to mate because female Huntsman spiders are not aggressive towards their male counterparts. When the female becomes aware that they are pregnant; what they do at least a couple of weeks before laying their eggs is that they work to enlarge the space inside their burrow.

They have some level of intelligence

Despite of the Huntsman spider's poor eyesight, they are also considered as quite smart for an invertebrate. This is because they are well aware of their surroundings and rely on their agile skills and very quick accurate fangs to defend themselves. These are enough proof that these species have some form of intelligence and is very capable of handling their surroundings and looking after themselves. Teenage spiders or juvenile Huntsman tend to choose lairs under

Chapter Five: Handling the Huntsman and Common Behaviors

rocks or fallen logs where they spend the majority of their time dodging predators, hunting smaller prey to dine on.

Tips for Handling Huntsman Spiders

Handling or interacting with your pet Huntsman can definitely provide a thrilling experience for you as the keeper but again as much as possible try not to handle them because if you do that they can get stressed and cause them to be ill. Consider the following steps:

Tip #1: Try not to get bitten! Accept the fact that there's a huge possibility that you'll get bitten but the good thing is that you can always protect yourself by being extra careful, and perhaps getting a glove on before you try to handle them. However, you have to also understand that Huntsman spiders really don't bite or is aggressive in any way if you ever attempt to hold them. They might be a bit wary and will literally jump away from you but once they get the hang of it, you can slowly let them crawl into your hand.

Chapter Five: Handling the Huntsman and Common Behaviors

Tip#2: Make sure to check its current move. The best way is to use a stick or a tong, you can slightly brush them or like use the equipment to touch their legs so that you can gauge their behavior at the moment, and perhaps let your spider know you're trying to do something.

Tip #3: Use your hand as a wall they can crawl or climb into. Once you've you can then slowly coax it out of the container, and place your hand near the container where it can walk right through.

Tip#4: Slowly pick them up with your fingers. Put your fingers or hands underneath their legs because in this way your spider is cradled, and you're not grabbing them like a predator. This technique may work only for some Huntsman.

Tip #5: Be patient. Spiders don't like the feeling of human hand because it's something foreign to them so be patient. Make sure to also notice how they'll react whenever you're grabbing them so that you'll have an idea how to handle them better. Don't try to force them if they don't want to be handled at the moment.

Chapter Five: Handling the Huntsman and Common Behaviors

Tip #6: Keep them safe. Make sure that whenever you're holding them, you keep them near the ground because they'll try to jump and get away from you. It will prevent them in falling from great heights. After handling and playing with them, carefully place them back inside their cage or enclosure.

Just a Reminder:

- Spiders like the Huntsman species are really not meant to be handled. It's mostly a pet you keep for observation. They don't benefit from handling, and they really don't care if you handle them or not

- They are quite social creatures compared to other spider species but it doesn't mean they're social to humans just like ordinary household pets.

- Spiders usually shy away even from their own kind. They'll try to get away from you because it's their natural instincts in the wild, so better get used to it.

- Keep in mind that your job is to keep them safe and provide them with everything they need including your attention. You can interact with them even without handling them, just checking in on them

Chapter Five: Handling the Huntsman and Common Behaviors

every day is more than enough for your long – legged friend.

Chapter Five: Handling the Huntsman and Common Behaviors

Chapter Six: Feeding Your Huntsman Spiders

When it comes to feeding your Huntsman spiders, the best strategy is to choose a certain day or time. Sticking to the schedule is more ideal for you and your pet spider because you can make sure that he/she is being fed at a consistent frequency. Most spiders have a slow metabolism which is why even if for some reason you forgot to feed them, they can still survive a couple of days without eating. It's highly recommended that you stick to a certain feeding routine so that your pet Huntsman will also get used to it and won't have a hard time adjusting.

It's also best that you ask the breeder where you bought the species regarding the feeding schedule, how

Chapter Six: Feeding Your Huntsman Spiders

much to feed, how to adjust, and what prey is best for your pet when it hits a certain age. This chapter will guide you on how to properly feed your Huntsman spider. Providing them with the right amount of nutrition will keep them strong and healthy against diseases.

Nutrition for your Huntsman Spiders

Feeding Adults

Huntsman spiders aren't the choosy kind of creatures. They will eat any insect or animal prey that they think they can tackle and kill in the wild. Just like humans, they do have favorite foods as well including roaches, beetles, moths, and grasshoppers. Slings usually feed on small – size insects but adult spiders can hunt and kill other creatures larger than them including other spider species. Having said this, Huntsman spiders will naturally just take care of themselves and they'll eventually eat the food you give them so you don't have to worry about feeding the 'wrong diet' because for these cannibalistic creatures, there's no such thing! Feed your adult Huntsman with 2 or 3 whole size roaches per week. Adjust if necessary.

Chapter Six: Feeding Your Huntsman Spiders

Feeding Slings

When it comes to feeding slings or baby spiders, they tend to grow quite rapidly in just a matter of weeks, they'll molt and then they'll double in size up until a certain point where they can start taking care of themselves and start taking down larger preys. Most keepers find that after putting a couple of flies or other small – size roaches in the enclosure, the baby Huntsman spiders seem to know or they seem to sense where these prey are located no matter how small they may be. Feed your baby Huntsman spiders with just a 1or 2 small insects per week. Adjust as they grow into juvenile spiders.

Feeding Frequency

Once you've already prepared the prey, and you have already decided what day or time to feed your pets, the next thing to do is to give it to them. What you can do is to simply drop the food inside their enclosure using some tools (which we will discuss later on) right in the spot where your spider is located so that you can later check back on it. If the flies or insects are gone then you'll know that your spider have already eaten them.

Keep in mind that you don't have to feed them daily, once or twice a week will do.

Chapter Six: Feeding Your Huntsman Spiders

Dos and Don'ts of Feeding

Do try to gut – load the prey. This works best for feeding adult Huntsman spiders. You can just slowly put in larger preys like roaches, and insects that are gut loaded with necessary nutrients. Once you've successfully placed it in, and you've seen your spider devour it with its mighty fangs, you can be sure that it's filled with the nutrients they need to be healthy.

Do mist their enclosure every day to avoid dehydration. The only way that these creatures drink is through your daily misting. Keep them hydrated by misting their enclosure and the substrate at least once or twice a day. You can use the squeeze bottle to pour in a bit of water in there. Never mist the spider directly! Just spray a bit of water into the walls of the enclosure and in the substrate so that the cage will not be too humid for them.

Do not leave uneaten prey inside the enclosure or container. If the prey is still there, it's better if you just pull it out and offer a fresh roach or insect.

Do not force them to eat if they don't want to. If you notice your spider refusing to eat, it could mean that they are getting ready to molt. You don't need to worry too much

Chapter Six: Feeding Your Huntsman Spiders

about it but just keep an eye and monitor him from time to time. Generally, they'll find their prey and eat it when they feel like doing so. Never ever force the food to them using your tool or even your hand because they might be threatened by you and become defensive.

Don't put a water dish inside the enclosure especially for sling spiders. You shouldn't try to put a small water dish in the enclosure especially if they're still young and small because they can drown in it. They usually get hydrated through the substrate or the walls of their enclosure/container since the humidity should be a bit higher when you're housing baby spiders otherwise they'll dry out very quickly.

Do monitor your pet's feeding behavior especially during molting season. Feeding them could be a rewarding experience. Just keep in mind that if they don't take the food, you have to understand that they probably just finished molting that's why they're not ready to take down food; it's the same thing if they're preparing for their molting season because they wouldn't want to take in live preys.

Chapter Six: Feeding Your Huntsman Spiders

Materials to Use When Feeding Huntsman Spiders

Since Huntsman spiders are quite agile creatures, you might want to use some tools that can help you to easily feed them without you getting bitten. As you now know, they're a 'sit and wait' predator, and they rely on their speed and reach to feed themselves in the wild. Hand feeding them might not be a good idea especially if you have an adult spider. Protect yourself by using the tools below:

- **Catch Container:** You can use this if ever your spider tries to escape during feeding time. Most spiders tend to stay inside their enclosure where it is safe, but there could be instances where they will try to flee away, so that's the reason why you need to have a catch cup around just in case.

- **Pair of Tweezers:** You should have a pair of bent nose tweezers that you can use for your sling spiders. This is a great tool because you can easily control it and it's also small which is perfect for handling tiny insects like roaches that you need later on. You can also use a larger set of tongs that you can use for your Huntsman spider once they get fully grown or use it to feed larger insects. Some breeders also use long tweezers for their aggressive eaters, if in case you

Chapter Six: Feeding Your Huntsman Spiders

have an aggressive Huntsman spider, this will keep your hands safe so that your spider won't mistake it as food.

- **Scientific Squeeze Bottles:** Never use large spray bottles because it tends to spook the spider and will cause them to ball up. What you can use is a scientific squeeze bottle that you can buy from pet stores, sport centers or Amazon and other online shops. The reason for this is that the squeeze bottles are very precise in putting in the water exactly where you want it, and also minimize the risk of spraying too much on your spider. The squeeze bottles have hoses that are very precise in squirting water. Spray bottles can be a major problem especially when you're dealing with slings or baby spiders because they tend to be more skittish and they'll try to escape or hide away inside their cave and may take a long while before they come out.

- **Paint Brush:** You can keep a paint brush around just so you can coax your pet if ever he/she tries to escape. The bristles on the soft brush tends to not irritate or scare off your spider, which is why it's a perfect handy dandy tool to keep them under controlled without threatening them. If you use your tongs or tweezers or things that are hard like metal tools, it

Chapter Six: Feeding Your Huntsman Spiders

usually causes them to panic and be in an attack mode.

Chapter Seven: Breeding Your Huntsman Spiders

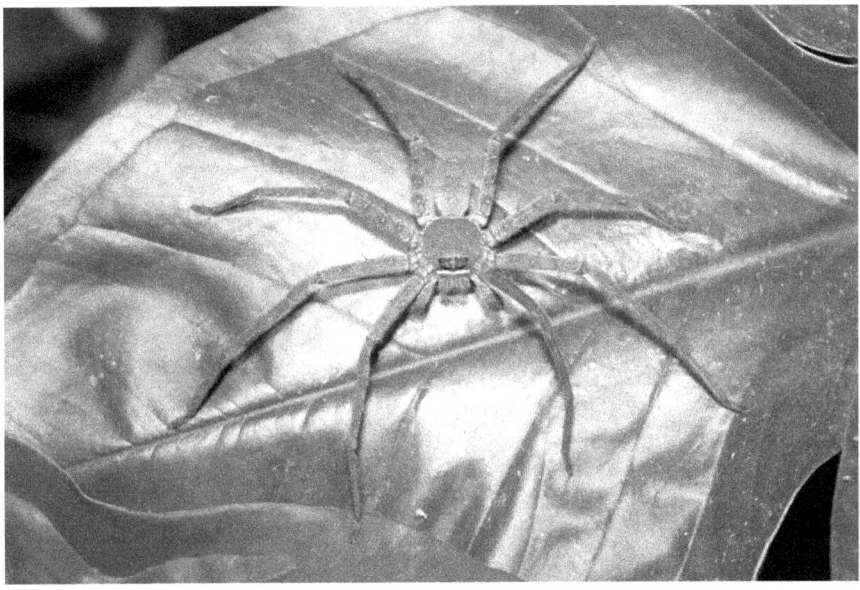

If you want to become full time spider hobbyists then breeding them yourself is the way to go. However, you have to consider lots of things, and it's not something that newbies should do. Breeding spiders is not easy because even if they don't really grow into large sizes compared to household pets, the newborns will need to be taken care of including their mother. They need to be well – fed, and be provided with all the nutrients they need. You need to exercise proper husbandry practices as well, and you need to know the basics of raising slings. Take note of the following tips and processes you'll learn in this chapter.

Chapter Seven: Breeding Your Huntsman Spiders

Tips to Prepare Your Huntsman Spider for Breeding

Identify the sex of your spiders and pair them up with healthy species. Unhealthy specimens will yield unhealthy offspring. Identify that the spiders being paired are sexually mature and capable of breeding and production. A healthy male should be placed in the terrarium of an equally healthy female.

Take note of the female heat cycle. Female Huntsman spiders have heat cycles so they usually accept a male during their heat cycle but not before the molting season.

Make sure that your female Huntsman is well fed. If you don't want your male spider to get eaten (because females are usually larger than males) then make sure to keep their stomach full.

Introduce the female and male before you pair them up. The good thing about female Huntsman spiders is that they're not aggressive towards their male counterparts compared to other spider species, and it's probably because they are quite communal creatures. However, precaution is still essential because they can still eat one another. There are many breeders who suggest that it's better if you put the female into the male's enclosure because then the female will

Chapter Seven: Breeding Your Huntsman Spiders

not think about food or eating the male since it's in a new environment, and it could make her slightly less aggressive. The other way around is to put the male or introduce the male spider to the female's lair. Introduce them and see how they react with one another.

Make sure that they are in a flat surface to avoid getting injured. What you want to do is put them down on the ground or in a flat surface where they won't hurt themselves if they fall or jump out of the enclosure. You can also put them in their own open containers and just get it near each other so that they can have a sense of mating. It might be ideal to use a catch cup to introduce the male to the opposite end of the enclosure where the female is.

Don't disturb your spiders once you see them trying to mate. As soon as the male and female successfully mount one another, you'll see an instant response. Once the male stops walking, it means that it can sense that a female is around through its sensory hairs, mouth or pheromones.

Never try to mate a spider when they're about to go through the molting stage. If you're going to breed them in captivity, make sure that you don't put in a female Huntsman spider with a male spider that's currently

Chapter Seven: Breeding Your Huntsman Spiders

molting because this can be dangerous since the molting stage is where all spiders are vulnerable to predation because they are defenseless at this stage. You can give the spiders around a few weeks after the final molting period so that the males can properly produce a sperm web, after that they can mate with one another. The molting stage often occurs once a year; every five years for male spiders, and a continuous process for female spiders.

The Mating Process

The Courtship

- Males usually seek out females at night since they are nocturnal creatures so don't expect them to mate during the day like what other species do. This is because in the wild, these animals are a lot more secure at night from potential predators than day are in the day.

- The male Huntsman spiders would purposely seek out female spiders that have hidden themselves to some dark location. The males would then entice the female out to make them interested.

Chapter Seven: Breeding Your Huntsman Spiders

- If the male Huntsman species like to mate with a virgin female, what they usually do is that they find quite younger or immature females and then guard them until they reach sexual maturity.

- Male spiders begin a display of courtship by raising its abdomen or the bulky area of their body while lowering the front of its body. It would shake its pedipalps or legs as it moves back and forth.

- An interested female will accept its advances willingly while an unreceptive one might ignore the male Huntsman or could also attack them (on rare occasions).

The Ritual

- The mating ritual involves the male drumming its pedipalps and the female drums back, or he'll do a periodic tapping.

- If for some reason, both your spiders are ignoring one another, you can use the chopstick to get some silk from the females in its pedipalps, and then let the male sort of sniff it or get it into its mouth so that

Chapter Seven: Breeding Your Huntsman Spiders

there can be some kind of reaction and excite the male to get them both into the mood.

The Mating

- Monitor your spiders while they are mating. However, try not to make any sudden moves or noises or breathe into them.

- Pick them up once the mating is over. It will usually just take a few minutes though some Huntsman spiders tend to last longer.

- After mating, the males would usually hold back the fangs of the female with its legs.

- Some breeders choose to mate a female with two healthy males to ensure absolute mating success. Keep in mind that this procedure will take up your time which is why if you're not serious about it, then maybe it's not a wise idea to push through.

Chapter Seven: Breeding Your Huntsman Spiders

Incubation and Egg – Laying

- After a couple of weeks, you can expect your female Huntsman is already expecting! Usually, female spiders will lay 40 to 50 eggs into its sac that measures about three centimeters in diameter. This sac will be stored in a burrow and the eggs are protected by a sturdy cover of silk webbing. The mother will guard its sac against potential predators.

- The slings or baby Huntsman will experience their first molt while they are in the sac. They then leave the sac and molt a second time before leaving the safety of their mom. Sometimes though, since Huntsman species are communal, the slings only leave their colony when they reach a certain age of maturity. In the wild, the babies still spend time with their older brothers and sisters because the older ones share prey to the younger siblings at least until they reach adulthood.

Chapter Seven: Breeding Your Huntsman Spiders

Chapter Eight: Frequently Asked Questions

In this chapter, we'll tackle and answer some of the most frequently asked questions of newbie keepers regarding how to keep spiders. The most commonly asked questions usually involved spider illnesses, husbandry, and the molting process. Hopefully, this chapter will help you and clarify some other spider keeping concerns that you may have.

Chapter Eight: Frequently Asked Questions

Frequently Asked Questions

What are other common illnesses of spiders?

Aside from molting problems, and dehydration, the most common are mites or parasite infestations. Since parasites are really microscopic in size, they usually find their way into the spider's enclosure (usually because of improper husbandry practices). When it does, it will pose great danger to the survival and health of your Huntsman spider. Be sure to remove dead insect carcasses from the enclosure using your tongs to avoid being mistaken as an intruder, and prevent from the spread of parasites coming from uneaten/left – over prey.

What happens if my spider loses a limb?

First of all, it's not unusual and impossible for these spiders to loose limbs. Don't panic when this happens. The molting stage that a spider goes through works like magic and this process allows them to regenerate lost limbs. You can also bring them to the vet so that you can have an idea of how to assist your pet.

Chapter Eight: Frequently Asked Questions

What if my spider gets dehydrated?

Most spiders including the Huntsman prefer to live in burrows, crevices, and hidden places which have higher humidity levels than the air outside. These spiders get their moisture from the prey they feed on. Spiders may seem to go on for days without taking a drink, but once they do, it is an indication that they are in need of water or perhaps they are quite dehydrated. This is why misting their enclosure every day is essential because they can also drink from the droplets of water, and it will also help in cooling off the humid environment inside the enclosure preventing them to become too dehydrated. Too much humidity is the main culprit in the stability of the environment of the spider. The humidity levels in the enclosure should be stable and within limits otherwise it will dry up your spider and it can be fatal for them.

What if my spider got some skin/ body injuries?

Some owners tend to see skin injuries or problems with their eight legged friend especially the abdominal area, what you can do is to bring your pet to the vet and have it checked. The blood of a spider is called hemolymph and it appears as white, pale, and blue - colored liquid. Careful application of the super glue can help your pet see another season, and molting will help it regenerate new parts. If ever your pet spider is injured due to mishap or a fall, you can simply aid it with super glue as it will help mend and clot the flow of blood preventing blood loss. This is an essential item that a spider hobbyist like you should have as first aid kit.

What if my spider experiences difficulty in molting?

Unhealthy and older spiders are quite prone to having difficulty in the molting process. You may actually notice your pet with a shorter leg compared to the other limbs. You may also detect lesser hair growth. Proper husbandry practices and proper nutrition will solve this problem. However, the natural process of invertebrate molting can still be a problem to some spiders that are nearing their lifespan. If ever your spider is already 2 years old and up, they're already considered as seniors, and difficulty in molting may already happen.

How does the molting process works?

There are usually stages that spiders go through during their molting process. See the following stages below so that you'd be familiar with them:

Chapter Eight: Frequently Asked Questions

Stage 1:

- This is the stage where your pet is still eating normally.

- This is where your pet is doing their usual routines and still quite active.

- Notice that the abdomen skin of the spider is pale which is in its normal shade.

- This is the point where your spider is starting to develop a new exoskeleton beneath its old exoskeleton. This is how they grow, and as these exoskeleton starts to develop, eventually the spider will eat enough, its body will then send out hormone signals that tells the spider that's it's time to stop eating. That's the only time you'll start to see some behavioral changes.

Stage 2:

- This is when the molt is imminent. The spider's body will start pumping fluids in the 2 sets of its exoskeletons to get the body ready to molt.

Chapter Eight: Frequently Asked Questions

- This is the point where your spider is ready to fully undergo through the molting process. You'll notice that the skin will become dark especially its abdominal area, and you may also see fluids leaking from its joints.

- This is also the point where they will start to lay down molting mats.

Stage 3:

- This is the part where your spider will expand itself to pop its limbs and work its way out of the molt.

- This process can take many hours to at least a day depending on the current size and age of your pet spider.

- This is the point where your pet is very vulnerable. Never touch or disturb them during this stage.

Stage 4:

- This is the stage where the Huntsman spider is already folding its new exoskeleton.

Chapter Eight: Frequently Asked Questions

- This is the stage where you'll see the skin filling out and hardening, you'll also see it stretching out.

- The fangs at this point is delicately soft that's why it won't be able to eat. Make sure to wait for at least a few days to a couple of weeks before you offer them food.

- During this stage, your spider can lose a lot of its moisture and can get dehydrated, so make sure that its enclosure or substrate is moist and well hydrated.

Chapter Eight: Frequently Asked Questions

Chapter Nine: Top 10 Spider Myths

Arachnophobia is perhaps the most common fears of most humans, and one of the main reasons why is because spiders are among the least 'human – looking' creatures. Needless to say, their body structure, their eight eyes, and eight hairy long legs as well as their agile and unpredictable moves are really not that attractive and 'pet worthy' for most people, so to speak. Spiders have long been one of the reasons why people shriek out of nowhere.

According to some people, the fear of spiders or other similar looking creatures is something that was passed on by our ancestors since they have no knowledge of what these eight legged bugs are, and perhaps the fear is already built

Chapter Nine: Top 10 Spider Myths

in our genetics. However, the reason why most people hate or are really afraid of them is because of useless rumors about spiders. Some myths and misconceptions are somewhat designed to make people even more scared than they already are. Usually, the reason why we're afraid is because of these false misconceptions, but nothing could be further from the truth.

Number 10: All Spiders Spin Webs!

Believe it or not, only about half of the spider species use their webs to catch their prey like small insects, roaches etc. Spiders like the Huntsman hunt for their food and also use their speed and agility, while other species like Wolf Spiders stalk their target food, and some only use their webs to sense vibrations of a potential prey or predator. There are a lot of spider species that don't spin webs, and more so at people. They only use it to transfer from one location to another, and perhaps when they need to defend themselves against larger predators. The reason why people assume every spider species spin webs and even shoot them at people is because we always come across a spider web, but as you know, the webs aren't dangerous at all. They're like cotton candy actually, and don't worry, if you're not the Green Goblin from Spiderman movies, no spider will ever try to shoot a web at you.

Chapter Nine: Top 10 Spider Myths

Number 9: There Are Spiders In Your Hair!

This myth was once popular around the 1950's because of a beehive hairstyle. Back then, people think that spiders will sort of nest into this type of hairdo because the beehive or bouffant hairstyle is really difficult to achieve which is why women who have this kind of hair would not often wash or comb it, thus the reason for spider infestation. If you really think about it, spiders can create a lair in your thick hair but the thing is they really don't want to hang out in any hair! They're not parasites! First of all, it'll be hard for them to move around your hair regardless of your hairstyle, and second, they will always get disturb if they choose to set up camp in hairs. Keep in mind that spiders don't want to get disturb as much as possible; this is the reason why they are often found under loose barks, rock crevices, and narrow dark spaces. Even if they happen to land on your hair, they wouldn't think of staying there for long because they know you'll easily whip them.

Number 8: Spiders Can't Get Caught In Their Own Webs

Most people believe this is true because we often see flies, roaches, and small insects get caught up in a spider's web but never the spider themselves and that's maybe because spiders are immune to it. Well, that could check out but in reality, spiders are not really immune to their own

Chapter Nine: Top 10 Spider Myths

webs, they just happen to be quite good at it and are very careful so as not to avoid getting stuck. Not all spider webs are sticky as well. Usually, spiders only do little web glues so that they themselves can avoid stepping on it, and even if they do, they know how to get out because they create spoke of webs that are not that sticky which they can walk into, the sticky ones are the circular threads which is the reason why lots of insects get caught. Spiders are a natural when it comes to web threading, it's not like they have magical powers or something.

Number 7: Spiders must be killed!

Animal experts always encourage everyone that whenever they see a spider, try not to whack it with a newspaper or your flip – flops. If you can hold it, just pick it up and let it go so that it can go back to its natural habitat. After all, these creatures don't intentionally want to trespass in your house, they just happen to wander inside. Some spiders however, have already evolved to an indoor lifestyle particularly in Europe, and that's probably because it's really freezing outside. This is the reason why there are lots of house spiders wandering around. House spiders are usually harmless to humans so there's nothing to worry about. If you don't want them to shock you because of their 'ugly' and freakish looks, just 'shoo' them away but don't kill it.

Chapter Nine: Top 10 Spider Myths

Keep in mind that they can help in reducing other pests inside your house, and spiders are an important part of the ecosystem.

Number 6: Spiders Can Lay Eggs under Your Skin

There have been some rumors circulating around that other people surprisingly believe, and it's a story about someone who went abroad and got bitten by a spider. When he came home, the bitten part starts swelling up, and when it popped, out came hundreds of tiny spiders. This is obviously not true, and perhaps only spread around for entertainment purposes but in reality, spiders don't lay eggs under people's skin. While it is true that some small animals like wasps can lay their eggs in an animal's skin, spiders can't lay their eggs in a human being or any other animal because there's no way it can inject the eggs, and they are very particular about where they lay their eggs. They usually lay eggs in dark and safe places away from any threat so that the eggs are protected.

Number 5: You're Never More Than 3 Feet from a Spider

Another myth that's just plain ridiculous! This myth started when Norman Platnick, an archaeologist, wrote an article around 1995 where he said the phrase "Where you sit as you read these lines, a spider is probably no more than a few yards away." Now because of that statement, and because he is an archaeologist, many people considered it as a fact, and around 2001, believe it or not, some books were quoting it as an actual fact when it's plainly speculation from Platnick. If you really think about it, there are more Hollywood stars that you can likely meet in Los Angeles than there are spiders 3 feet away from where you are.

Number 4: Black Widows Eat Their Mates

This myth has some fact into it but it's also completely misunderstood. As we've discussed in previous chapters, some spider species (with the exception of the Huntsman) do eat their mates or the male spiders after mating. This is why people coined a suspicious woman or evil woman a "black widow" in relation to the Black Widow Spider's behavior. However, this doesn't happen often, and not all species of Black Widow spiders eat their mates, the only time that they do is if they're really hungry, after all these creatures are cannibalistic in nature.

As we've discuss, male spiders are usually smaller in size than females regardless of the spider species. When spiders are mating, males have to be quite close to the female's mouth which is why sometimes if the female is really hungry; it's easier for them to just take a bite off of

Chapter Nine: Top 10 Spider Myths

their partner. Even if there's some truth to this, you have to understand that this is their nature, and it's not right to fear these spiders because of their natural inclination.

Number 3: You Swallow an Average of Eight Spiders a Year

This is one of the most popular spider misconceptions, and it's because of Lisa Holst. She's the one responsible for spreading such myth for experimental purposes. The experiment is that she wanted to demonstrate that lots of people believe almost anything they read online. To test her hypothesis, she sends out fake facts via email including this myth. As it turns out, she made her point over a million times, and lots of people accepted this fake fact that people swallow spiders during sleep. Holst got the myth from a book called "Insect Fact and Folklore," unfortunately; it became widespread and was passed on to many people, which is also the reason why some people are scared of spiders. Think about it, why in the world would spiders go directly to your mouth, when it knows you are an absolute threat to them, and you're way larger and powerful? Unless, they're committing suicide, they would never go near your mouth.

Chapter Nine: Top 10 Spider Myths

Number 2: That thing with "Daddy Longlegs"

The Pholcid house Spider is usually the spider species that's referred to as "daddy longlegs" and it's true that Pholcid house spider has some mild venom, but it is considered harmless to humans even if you actually get bitten by it. There's also no such thing as daddy longlegs because lots of other creatures also go by this name. Species like crane fly are not even spiders but sometimes because of the term daddy longlegs, they become a spider species and are also feared.

Number 1: The Killer "Camel Spiders"

Perhaps the most famous of all the spider myths is Camel Spiders. Unfortunately, "camel spiders" are not even spiders to begin with! This is another myth that circulated via email a few years back when an arachnid called the Iraqi Camel Spider that's claimed to be 1 foot in length, runs at 25 meters per hour, hide's on a camel's stomach, creates a screeching noise when it runs, and is very dangerous because its venom already killed a soldier. This is all false! Camel spiders are part of the arachnid family but it is a solifugid species. Its body structure looks like a scorpion and a spider but it's not considered a spider at all! These camel spiders don't even grow more than 6 inches, and they can't even run that fast!

Chapter 10: Summary and Care Sheet

Keeping Huntsman spiders even for those of you who already have a prior experience can still be quite challenging but also rewarding. You get to take care of these creatures, save yourself from lots of other pests, and also help the ecosystem as a whole. Not to mention the fact that you can look cool to your friends because you are taking care of this giant, long – legged, and fearsome spider. As a responsible keeper, it's your job to also inform and perhaps correct others who are afraid of the Huntsman spider because of false information. It's now your job to show them that even how friendly and sociable this spider can be, and how most of the time, they're really just trying to be themselves.

Chapter Ten: Summary and Care Sheet

Common Types of Huntsman Species

- Brown Huntsman Spider (*Heteropoda jugulans*)
- Badge Huntsman spider (*Neosparassus spp.*)
- Green Huntsman spider (*Typostola barbata*)
- Grey Huntsman spider (*Holconia immanis*)

Physical Features

- Huntsman spiders are large, with a flattened body structure, and laterally spread out banded legs. They have leg joints that are rotated backwards making the underside of their legs face forward.

- The body of adult Huntsman spider measures 2.2 to 2.8 centimeters, or about one inch. Their leg span measures 3 to 5 inches or around 7 to 12 centimeters.

- There's also a carpet of hair located on the underside of the last joints of their long legs as well as in the tips of their feet enabling them to grip on flat surfaces.

- They can climb sheer vertical surfaces without falling, thanks to their crab – like legs.

- Both male and females possess a yellow to cream clypeus, and they have a band that encircles their carapace. The band is usually color tan in females, and cream – colored in makes.

Behavioral Characteristics

- When it comes to mating, Huntsman spiders tend to have the longest mating time compared to most spider species

- When it comes to reproduction, when the female Huntsman is ready to lay her eggs, what she'll do is spin a silk pad. She will then lay the hundreds of blue – green colored eggs into a hard web sac that she created, similar to a nest.

- Some huntsman spiders tend to be quite social as well compared to most species which are cannibalistic. They live in groups sometimes and usually defend their colony against other spider species.

Chapter Ten: Summary and Care Sheet

- They are strong, fast, agile, and has powerful jaws which they all use to capture their prey. And like many spiders, they kill their prey buy injecting venom into it and sucking blood before completely consuming them

- Some creatures are cold – sensitive, and some thrive in warmer areas. They can also adapt very well to human habitat, this is why they can be seen in sheds, roofs, barns, and other sheltered areas.

- Huntsman spiders are nocturnal species. They are known as ambush predators, and they don't use their webs to catch their prey, instead what they do is to sit and wait before leaping onto their target food.

- Sit and Wait Predator. Another reason why Huntsman spiders use to detect if a prey is nearby is through their vision and vibrations. Even if their vision is not as accurate as what us humans possess it still works out for them in combination of the vibrations they feel through the hairs on their eight legs.

Chapter Ten: Summary and Care Sheet

- Agile at night, timid during the day. In daytime, Huntsman spiders are considered timid unless they are taunted or threatened. If there's no one bothering them or if a prey is not around, they usually just stay and rest under rock crevices, loose tree barks, and other dark retreats.

- A bit of a biter but not dangerously venomous. Huntsman spiders almost never bite even if they have a reputation of being a biter. They usually rely on their speed to get away from potential predators but even if they do bite you, you have nothing to worry about because usually it's just a quick nip to defend themselves but they don't usually inject their mild venoms.

- Discreet and shy – type creatures. Spiders in general are discreet creatures, which is why little is known regarding their communication methods. They usually meet with other species of their own kind during the mating season.

- They have some level of intelligence. Despite of the Huntsman spider's poor eyesight, they are also considered as quite smart for an invertebrate. This is because they are well aware of their surroundings and rely on their agile skills and very quick accurate fangs to defend themselves.

Taxonomy: Kingdom Animalia, Phylum Arthropoda, Class Arachnida, Order Araneae, Family Sparassidae.

Distribution: The Huntsman spider is believed to have originated in Sri Lanka, and southern regions of India but majority are now distributed in many regions of Australia, and even in warm areas like Florida, U.S.A. They can also be found in subtropical areas of United States like California, Florida, Texas, Georgia and coastal areas of South Carolina. They can also be found in some parts of Asia as some of its relatives are distributed there.

Habitat: These spiders are fond of entering houses and buildings but they're usually found in rock crevices, under loose barks of trees, tight and narrow spaces, dark hidings.

Chapter Ten: Summary and Care Sheet

Benefits of Getting Pet Permit

- Licenses ensure that the populations of wild plants and animals like the Huntsman spider remain viable.

- It helps maintain in keeping, taking, using and transport of wildlife for recreational, commercial or other purposes.

- It protects illegal collection of this species from the wild by illegal traders.

Pros and Cons of Keeping a Huntsman Spider

They are Big and Really Agile: Native Australian creatures can run up to 42 body lengths per second, while some only run for about 16 body lengths per second on average.

They have a Long Lifespan: Huntsman spiders are one of the long – lived spider species out there. On average they can live of up to 2 ½ years.

Some Huntsman species are communal: There are social Huntsman species that can live in complex family groups. They can live with other 150 of their kind and is led by a dominant matriarch.

Chapter Ten: Summary and Care Sheet

Reminders When Choosing Where to Buy

Step #1: Ask for recommendations. It's best to read testimonials of people who have already bought spiders from specific breeders.

Step #2: Compare the recommended breeders. You can check the recommended breeders' purchase cost, their background or About Page (if any) on their website, and see who best resonates with you.

Step #3: Compare the purchase prices and check their current stock. Never order a spider online without asking where it came from especially if the cost seems unusually high.

Step #4: Go and visit the breeder and the spider breeds! This way, it will validate or further verify your assumptions, and you'll see the spiders live in action.

Step #5: Ask for proof from the breeder. You should ask for pictures of the breed, and if possible a video to see if you're getting the right breed.

Step #6: Be inquisitive. One sure way of knowing if the breeder you've chosen really knows what he/she is doing is through asking them questions.

Chapter Ten: Summary and Care Sheet

Do's and Don'ts of Choosing a Huntsman Spider

- Do buy a Huntsman that displays alertness and agility.
- Don't buy a Huntsman that is curled up.
- Do consider your budget.
- Do consider your time and attention.
- Don't buy a lethargic Huntsman.
- Don't buy unhealthy looking Huntsman.
- Do Your Own Due Diligence.

Housing HuntsmanSpiders

- Buy a slightly tall enclosure for your arboreal pet.
- Adjust the size of the enclosure according to their age.
- Huntsman spiders are communal.
- Make sure to get a durable enclosure.
- Buy a glass tank.
- Provide your pet with substrate.
- Set up rock crevices and loose flat barks inside the cage.
- Decorate your spider's enclosure.
- Provide heat pads and thermometers.

Chapter Ten: Summary and Care Sheet

- Regulate the temperature and humidity levels.
- Mist the enclosure every day.
- Remove any unnecessary left – overs like food or exoskeleton after molting.
- Check in on them from time to time.

Handling Tips

- Tip #1: Try not to get bitten!
- Tip #2: Make sure to check its current move.
- Tip #3: Use your hand as a wall they can crawl or climb into.
- Tip #4: Slowly pick them up with your fingers.
- Tip #5: Be patient.
- Tip #6: Keep them safe.

Heads Up!

- Spiders like the Huntsman species are really not meant to be handled. It's mostly a pet you keep for observation. They don't benefit from handling, and they really don't care if you handle them or not

Chapter Ten: Summary and Care Sheet

- They are quite social creatures compared to other spider species but it doesn't mean they're social to humans just like ordinary household pets.

- Spiders usually shy away even from their own kind. They'll try to get away from you because it's their natural instincts in the wild, so better get used to it.

- Keep in mind that your job is to keep them safe and provide them with everything they need including your attention. You can interact with them even without handling them, just checking in on them every day is more than enough for your long – legged friend.

Dos and Don'ts of Feeding

Do try to gut – load the prey. This works best for feeding adult Huntsman spiders. You can just slowly put in larger preys like roaches, and insects that are gut loaded with necessary nutrients.

Do mist their enclosure every day to avoid dehydration. The only way that these creatures drink is through your daily misting. Keep them hydrated by misting their enclosure and the substrate at least once or twice a day.

Chapter Ten: Summary and Care Sheet

Do not leave uneaten prey inside the enclosure or container. If the prey is still there, it's better if you just pull it out and offer a fresh roach or insect.

Do not force them to eat if they don't want to. If you notice your spider refusing to eat, it could mean that they are getting ready to molt.

Don't put a water dish inside the enclosure especially for sling spiders. You shouldn't try to put a small water dish in the enclosure especially if they're still young and small because they can drown in it.

Do monitor your pet's feeding behavior especially during molting season. Keep in mind that if they don't take the food, you have to understand that they probably just finished molting that's why they're not ready to take down food

Tips to Prepare Your Huntsman Spider for Breeding

- Identify the sex of your spiders and pair them up with healthy species.
- Take note of the female heat cycle.
- Make sure that your female Huntsman is well fed.

Chapter Ten: Summary and Care Sheet

- Introduce the female and male before you pair them up.
- Make sure that they are in a flat surface to avoid getting injured.
- Don't disturb your spiders once you see them trying to mate.
- Never try to mate a spider when they're about to go through the molting stage.

The Mating Process

The Courtship

Males usually seek out females at night since they are nocturnal creatures so don't expect them to mate during the day like what other species do.

The Ritual

The mating ritual involves the male drumming its pedipalps and the female drums back, or he'll do a periodic tapping.

The Mating

After mating, the males would usually hold back the fangs of the female with its legs. Some breeders choose to mate a female with two healthy males to ensure absolute mating success. Keep in mind that this procedure will take up your time which is why if you're not serious about it, then maybe it's not a wise idea to push through.

Incubation and Egg – Laying

- After a couple of weeks, you can expect your female Huntsman is already expecting! Usually, female spiders will lay 40 to 50 eggs into its sac that measures about three centimeters in diameter.

- Huntsman species are communal, the slings only leave their colony when they reach a certain age of maturity. In the wild, the babies still spend time with their older brothers and sisters because the older ones share prey to the younger siblings at least until they reach adulthood.

Index

A

acclimatization	83
Age of Sexual Maturity	102
aggressiveness	25, 66
Arachnid	2
arachnophobia	19
Arboreal	2

B

Bad molting	9, 91, 95
beginner tarantulas	7, 21
Bleeding and injuries	9, 91, 94
Book lungs	2
breeder	8, 40
breeding	9, 71, 73, 102

C

Carapace	3
CB	3
Cleaning Frequency	101
Clutch Size	103
costs	7, 15, 16, 18

D

Dehydration	9, 91
Diet	8, 18, 23, 24, 26, 28, 29, 31, 32, 35, 36, 38, 55, 56, 58, 102

E

Exoskeleton	3

F

Feeding	9, 2, 55, 68, 102, 129

G

Gestation Period	102
Glossary	7, 2
Gravid	3
Gut Loading Crickets	8, 57

H

Habitat Requirements	23, 24, 26, 28, 29, 31, 32, 34, 36, 38, 101
Handling	8, 15, 23, 25, 26, 28, 29, 31, 35, 61, 65
Health Conditions	8, 9, 52, 89, 91, 101
Honduran Curly Hair Tarantula (Brachypelma albopilosum)	8, 26
husbandry	60, 82

I

Incubation Period	103
injuries	94
Instar	3
Internal infection from mold and fungus	9, 91, 96
invertebrate	3

L

license	12, 19
Lifespan	8, 18, 23, 25, 26, 28, 29, 31, 33, 35, 36, 38, 101
Losing a leg	9, 91, 93

M

Mexican Redknee (Brachypelma smithi)	7, 25

Mexican Redleg (Brachypelma smithi)	7, 24
Molting	3, 9, 69, 70

N

Natural Habitat	23, 24, 26, 27, 29, 30, 32, 34, 36, 37

O

Origin	7, 8, 23, 24, 26, 27, 29, 30, 32, 34, 36, 37
other pets	14, 19
Oviparous	3

P

Parasites	9, 91, 97
Pedipalp	3
Primary Behavioral Characteristics	8, 101
Primary Diet	102
Pros and Cons	7, 17, 18

R

Recommended Equipment	101
Recommended Habitat	24, 26, 28, 29, 30, 34, 36, 38
Recommended Temperature	101
Regions of Origin	7, 100

S

Sexual Maturity among Males	9, 70
Size	23, 24, 26, 27, 29, 30, 32, 34, 36, 37
Size at Birth	103
Spinning Silk	9, 69
Startup costs	15

T

Temperature and Humidity Requirements   8, 51
Terrestrial   4

W

Water   102
wild caught   4

Photo Credits

Page 1 Photo by user Azonei via Flickr.com, https://www.flickr.com/photos/azonei/7978602247/

Page 5 Photo by user Jean and Fred via Flickr.com, https://www.flickr.com/photos/jean_hort/6940724227/

Page 17 Photo by user budak via Flickr.com, https://www.flickr.com/photos/budak/24949562128/

Page 28 Photo by user John Tann via Flickr.com, https://www.flickr.com/photos/31031835@N08/7161015535/

Page 37 Photo by user John Tann via Flickr.com, https://www.flickr.com/photos/31031835@N08/3437365043/

Page 46 Photo by user Jean and Fred via Flickr.com, https://www.flickr.com/photos/jean_hort/7460123782/

Page 55 Photo by user Rob Russell via Flickr.com, https://www.flickr.com/photos/gtveloce/5347265357/

Page 63 Photo by user budak via Flickr.com, https://www.flickr.com/photos/budak/30832703966/

Page 71 Photo by user raw spin via Flickr.com,

https://www.flickr.com/photos/8267212@N03/4255976617/

Page 79 Photo by user 及良 及影 via Flickr.com,

https://www.flickr.com/photos/33748728@N02/8164238160/in/photostream/

Page 88 Photo by user Frank Starmer via Flickr.com,

https://www.flickr.com/photos/spiderman/3844258740/

References

"10 Most Common Symptoms of Spider Bites" - Healthremediesjournal.com

http://healthremediesjournal.com/10-most-common-symptoms-of-spider-bites/

"Huntsman Spider" - Reptilepark.com.au

https://reptilepark.com.au/animals/spiders/australian-spiders/huntsman-spider/

"What Is The Huntsman Spider? How Big Is It? Does It Bite?" - Scienceabc.com

https://www.scienceabc.com/nature/animals/what-is-the-huntsman-spider-how-big-is-it-does-it-bite.html

"How to Make a Pet Tarantula Habitat You Can Be Proud Of" - Petful.com

https://www.petful.com/other-pets/how-make-pet-tarantula-habitat/

"How to Keep Spiders as Pets" - Boyslife.org

https://boyslife.org/hobbies-projects/funstuff/1282/how-to-keep-spiders-as-pets/

"Setting up a Pet Spider Enclosure" - Mypets.net.au

https://www.mypets.net.au/setting-up-a-pet-spider-enclosure/

"Everything You Wanted To Know About Huntsman Spiders (But Were Afraid To Ask)"- Lifehacker.com.au

https://www.lifehacker.com.au/2017/11/everything-you-wanted-to-know-about-huntsman-spiders-but-were-afraid-to-ask/

"Hidden housemates: Australia's huge and hairy huntsman spiders" – TheConversation.com

https://theconversation.com/hidden-housemates-australias-huge-and-hairy-huntsman-spiders-55017

"Huntsman Spider" - Animalcorner.co.uk

https://animalcorner.co.uk/animals/huntsman-spider/

"Huntsman Spiders" - Australianmuseum.net.au

https://australianmuseum.net.au/huntsman-spiders

"Huntsman Spiders" - Minibeastwildlife.com.au

http://www.minibeastwildlife.com.au/resources/huntsman-spiders/

"Hunting the Huntsman – Keeping the Giant Crab or Huntsman Spider – Part 2" – ThatPetPlace.com

http://blogs.thatpetplace.com/thatreptileblog/2009/12/30/hunting-the-huntsman-keeping-the-giant-crab-or-huntsman-spider-part-2/#.WyfwgapKi1s

"Huntsman Spider" – Wikipedia.org

https://en.wikipedia.org/wiki/Huntsman_spider

"Huntsman Spider" – Termite.com

http://www.termite.com/spiders/Huntsman-Spider.shtml

www.ingramcontent.com/pod-product-compliance
Lightning Source LLC
Chambersburg PA
CBHW071955070426
42453CB00008BA/801